HANDBOOKS OF EUROPEAN NATIONAL DANCES

EDITED BY
VIOLET ALFORD

DANCES OF POLAND

Plate 1   Mazur

DANCES of POLAND

HELEN WOLSKA

NOVERRE PRESS

COLOUR ILLUSTRATIONS BY
G. DOUGLAS HALLIDAY
ASSISTANT EDITOR
YVONNE MOYSE

First published in 1952
This edition published in 2021 by
The Noverre Press
Southwold House
Isington Road
Binsted
Hampshire
GU34 4PH

ISBN 978-1-914311-11-6

© 2021 The Noverre Press

CONTENTS

INTRODUCTION	Page 7
The Krakowiak	8
Polonez	10
Mazur	11
Zakopane	11
A Village Wedding	13
Music	14
Costume	15
When Dancing May Be Seen	18
THE DANCES	19
Poise of Body, Arm Gestures, Holds	20
Basic Steps	21
Krakowiak	23
Mazur	26
Góralski	30
Oberek	33
NOTE ON PRONUNCIATION	37
BIBLIOGRAPHY	38

Illustrations in Colour, pages 2, 12, 29, 39
Map of Poland, page 6

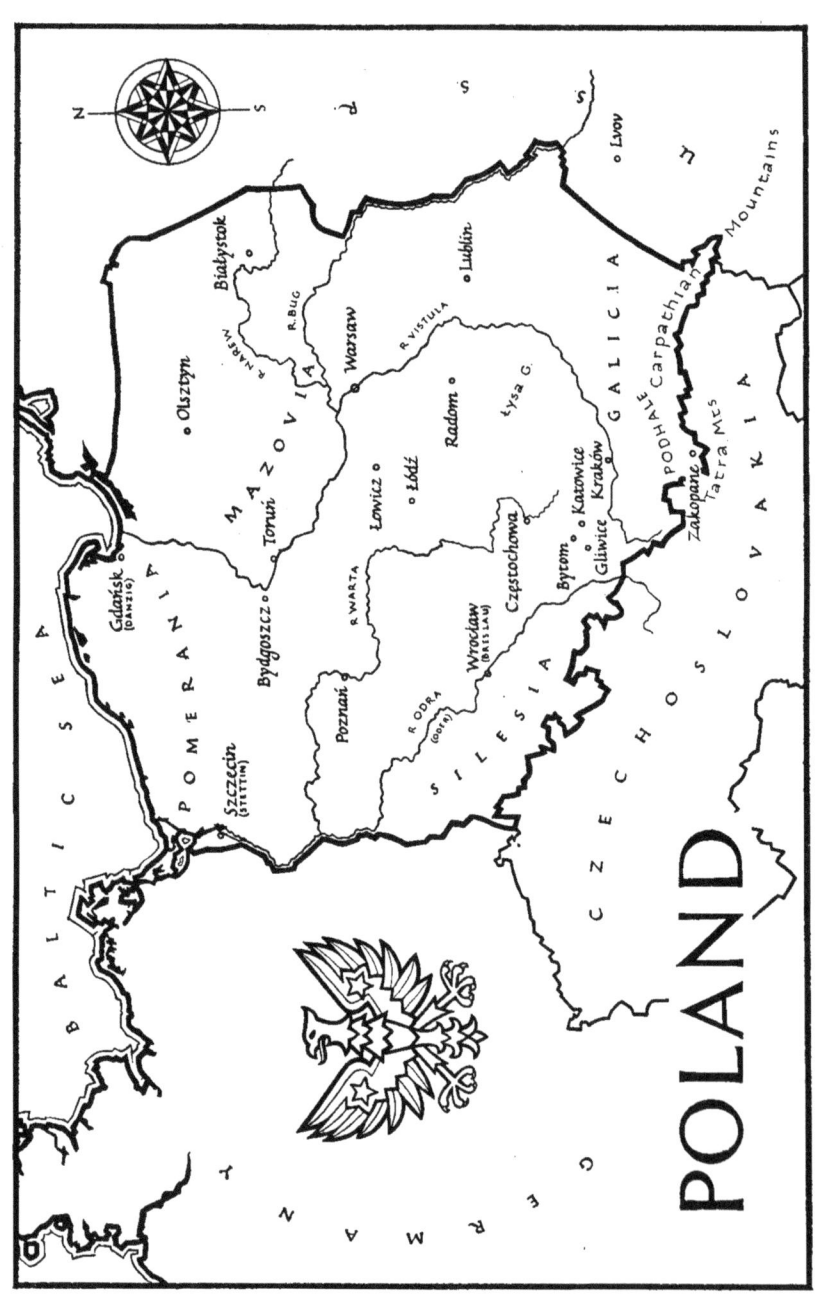

INTRODUCTION

Dancing has always been the recreation *par excellence* of the Polish people, our dances famous in history and in ballet, our dancers worthy of their traditional inheritance.

Our folk dances have had a continuous, robust life and are especially popular between Christmas and Easter when farm work is almost at a standstill, our winters being long and severe. Many of our dances have been lost to us in course of the centuries but we still possess a large number, indicative of our love of music and dancing.

Poland has had a troublous history, her geographical situation laying her open to perpetual movement between East and West. The country, so easily traversed, can be divided into regions fairly simple to delineate, and the dances of Poland can conveniently be related to these regions. Those of each geographical region have common characteristics.

From the Baltic southwards we have the Plain, the Forest Plateau Uplands and the Mountains; the first section, the Plain, having a subdivision known as the Baltic Heights, running from Pomerania through the Mazovian Lakes to White Russia. Heights rise to about 600 ft., and if a large-scale map is examined hundreds of tiny lakes will be discovered, remains of the Ice Age. This subdivision is a very little-developed area and not one to have originated dances.

The second region consists of the Silesian Hills, the Kraków Jura, the Galician Plateau, the Lysa Góra, the Lublin Hills and the Podolian Plateau. This region attains too great a height to be labelled a plain; Forest Plateau Uplands is an apt description.

The Plain furnishes the largest population and the greatest number of dances, including the Polonez (Polonaise), Łowiczanka, Mazur (Mazurka) and the showy Oberek. Two factors have allowed these dances to reach full development, the early settlement of this region and its vulnerability to outside influence—although there is surprisingly little evidence of such influence, which marks perhaps another manifestation of the Polish spirit of independence. For the second region Krakowiak and Silesian dances are more robust than those of the Plain but do not reach the liveliness and agility of the wild mountain dances such as the Góralski and the Harnas.

THE KRAKOWIAK

The Krakowiak and Kujawiak are examples of peasant dances in the rough, transformed by the Polish gentry into more finished and elegant forms. The Łowiczanka also was adapted from a folk dance of the district of Łowicz, while the celebrated Polonaise (of which more later) is possibly not of peasant origin at all. The Krakowiak, a very popular and lively dance, originated at Kraków (Cracow), and Kraków is named after the legendary Krak who slew a dragon and built the first city on the Wawel hill above the then swampy Vistula. This city remained Poland's capital until 1596. Here is the famous church of Our Lady (Marjacki or Panna Marja), where a trumpeter marks the hours by playing the tune called *hejnał*. When there were no clocks the citizens depended on this call to pause in their daily round and pray to the Protectress of the town. In 1241, when Batu Khan and his dreaded Tartars overran the country, the people fled for safety up the Wawel hill, but the trumpeter remained at his post down below bound by the oath which trumpeters take to this day. A Tartar arrow struck him as he was sounding his call. In memory of this long-ago hero the tune always stops short, cut off at the same uncompleted bar.

This historical trumpet call has been used very effectively to open a Polish ballet:

We have historical mention of the Krakowiak being danced in 1510, under King Sigismund. Compared with the Polonez it represents a less advanced social development, and is danced by many couples often standing round a circle, its music in a very marked 2/4 rhythm. It can also be performed by one couple with dramatic action and then is often danced, accompanied by singing, in an exciting and expressive way. The men wear a quantity of metal rings on the belt which jingle as they spring and strike their heels together.

The national dances of Poland show the men to great advantage. They perform with swagger and bravado—except in the Polonez which, full of polite and chivalrous manners, was never a folk dance.

The great difference between Polish and Russian dancing is seldom realised: the first showing men and women—whether peasants or aristocrats—dancing together; the second, largely based on Eastern notions, showing for the most part men and women dancing separately.

Three categories of Polish dances can be distinguished: those performed by the peasants, which are the true folk dances; those like the Mazur which have become ballroom dances; and our brilliant stage dances which may be stylised and highly developed folk dances as shown on the stage.

POLONEZ

This is *Taniec Polski;* the Polish Dance; *Polonaise* in French, *Polonäse* in German, and in Italian *Polacca*. It seems to be one of the oldest of our national dances and is perhaps the only dance not of folk origin. Tradition has it that it is derived from a procession of noblemen at the celebrations on the ascension of Henri III (of Valois) to the throne of Poland in 1573. Nevertheless tradition adds that the still older peasant dance Polski* was used as the foundation of this elaborate cortège.

Its French name probably came into use on this important occasion. The Polonez is still a procession rather than a dance properly speaking, and was often the opening item at aristocratic and Court balls. It is in moderate 3/4 time and suits the mature as well as the young. It displays several sides of the Polish character, is stately, grave and dignified and shows courtly etiquette allied to bravura. As time went on and its popularity in aristocratic and other circles gained ground, the composition of a new Polonez became the expected accompaniment to a great occasion, in much the same way as an English masque was produced for celebrations. The Kościuszko Polonez, 1792, was dedicated to a great patriot, while Chopin's Polonaise in A major is the perfect example of such composition. It has been used for dancing for over a hundred years and more lately has become almost a national anthem, being played in theatres and at official ceremonies. The Polish radio

---

* See the volumes on *Sweden, Finland* and *Denmark* in this series for the Polska in those countries.

used it in the terrible days of September 1939, to rally our spirits before the dreaded news.

Every State ball opened with a Polonez, officers wearing their uniforms, noblemen wearing their close-fitting velvet coats with voluminous sleeves, a magnificent coloured sash knotted in front, and top boots; over all a black or white satin cloak trimmed with fur, a fur cap with feathers completing the picture. At Court, as in any modest country house, the couples promenaded through all the rooms, to finish with a deep reverence to each other.

MAZUR

The Mazur or Mazurka is as well known as the Polonaise, for it travelled all over Europe and assumed a simple ballroom form, now long passed out of fashion. Originally it came from the province of Mazovia, a true folk dance for eight or sixteen couples in a circle. Skilful dancers indulged in much improvisation, so the dance was full of variety. It used to be sung; its chief characteristic is the strong accent on the second beat, and it is now often used as a stately dance to end a ball.

ZAKOPANE

As a rule Polish men and women dance together, but in the Tatra mountains, in the Podhale region around Zakopane, we find virile men's dances such as the Brigands' Dance, of which the Góralski (p. 30) is a short version. It used to be performed round a fire, the men facing inwards and beating the ground with their hatchets, *toporki*, which are carried to hack out footholds in mountain climbing. The bystanders join in the song which, as in all Góral dances, accompanies the dance. There are steps reminiscent of Cossack steps, leaps, waving of *toporki* and jumping over the fire. Old paintings show us dancers draining a flask of

Plate 2 Oberek

wine held in one hand and firing a pistol with the other. Leaping the fire seems to have been part of an initiation ceremony in the robber bands.

A VILLAGE WEDDING

If you have the good fortune to be invited to a wedding you will be summoned the day before the ceremony by young men with gay ribbons in their hats who, clicking their heels together at parting, say 'Stand with God'. To this you reply 'God lead you'. The house to which you go is made of wood, the chinks filled with wood shavings plaited together; in very old houses with moss. The sound of music comes from the house and you find several fiddlers playing on two- or three-stringed fiddles and a double-bass not much larger than a 'cello. Probably the players are gypsies. They are playing in the 'black room' where is the stove and where are benches decorated with holy pictures and paper cut in intricate patterns; the 'white room' now holds the bride with two maidens braiding her hair, singing the while. She is brilliantly dressed; there is constant bustle, and as constant refreshment; dancing begins, the bridegroom inviting the women guests. The men stamp vigorously, the gay skirts swirl in dazzling patterns. The girls dance in high laced boots, their Sunday footwear, or everyday shoes made of one piece of leather with a thong to wind round the leg.

During the evening each girl gives one of her shoes to be placed in a single file of footwear pointing towards the door. The girl whose shoe finds its place in the doorway will be the first betrothed.

This day is *dobra nocka*, 'good little night' or eve of the wedding. Until late at night there is feasting and dancing. Often there will be a humorous version of the Robbers' Dance in which one robber is killed but cannot be buried. When put in his grave his limbs will not remain in position:

when his legs lie together, his arms fly up; when his arms are secured, his legs spring wide open; so he is brought back to life and the dance ends in uproarious gaiety.

Next morning the guests dance the Krakowiak while waiting for the bridal pair. When the bride and bridegroom arrive they are greeted with bread and salt, which they eat together, and are then blessed by the bride's parents. Several groomsmen, young men carrying wands decorated with flowers at the top, help to order the proceedings at country weddings.

MUSIC

At village festivities the music is supplied by violins, 'cello, small double-bass, a drum of some sort and a flute. But the fiddle is the chosen instrument for accompanying dancing. Fiddles have two or three strings; if the 'cello is called in to strengthen them it is laid across the knees and the rhythm is tapped out on the belly of the instrument as though it were a drum. Sometimes there will be a dulcimer and the ubiquitous accordion. When calling a dance the men put money into the double-bass. They like to improvise verses to dance-airs, the leader beginning, the second man next and so on. In the Eastern Beskides we still see a primitive form of bagpipes. They must have been far more common than they are now, for a contemporary of Bach is quoted as stating, 'I have heard as many as thirty-six bagpipes and six violins played together'.

It is thanks to Dr. Chałubiński and the sanatorium he opened at Zakopane—which word literally means 'beyond cultivation'—that first the region and then its songs became known. The doctor discovered a mountain guide, one 'Sabata', who possessed a rich store of legends, tales and songs, many of which have been collected. The Góral dances are nearly all sung, onlookers joining in. Since then Paderewski published his Tatra Album of mountain airs.

Many composers have used our dance forms in their works. Bach did so, and his son Wilhelm Friedemann. The Mazurka with its strong accent on the second beat has been constantly used, especially by Stanisław Moniuszko, composer of the national opera *Halka*, and some very attractive Mazurkas (*Danses Masoviennes*) were written by Zygmunt Noskowski (op. 38). Again Karol Szymanowski was attracted by the music of the Tatra mountains and gave us the ballet *Harnasie*, which was produced with brilliancy in Paris by Serge Lifar. Of our greatest composer's Polonaises we have already spoken.

Our country has produced some famous ballet dancers, notable amongst whom are Idzikowski and Wojcikowski.

COSTUME

Our country boasts some of the most colourful and interesting costumes in Europe. None is 'national', all are regional, with details varying from village to village, so that in the Łowicz area, for example, it is as possible to place a man by the cut of his trousers as by his speech. To the south, trousers are generally plain, of near-white homespun material. In the uplands the women favour bright, plain colours for skirts and aprons. Skirts are made everywhere from home-grown flax, damped and bleached white in the sun. When we climb into the mountains, dress changes and we come to the celebrated Góral costume.

Góralski. For this dance is worn one of our outstanding costumes, developed on the mountain heights. The men's trousers are of coarse white wool turning with age to shades of brown. They are very tight, and show a stripe of blue wool down the outside of each leg and two tufts of red wool at the ankles. On the front of the thigh is the traditional embroidery called *parzenica*. The belt is studded with brass tacks; it served the brigands as an armoury, carrying their pistols and knives. It is now worn by the head shepherd of the high communal pastures as the insignia of his authority over the *juhasi* or young shepherds. Every man must possess a sheepskin jacket, and these are worn (often cloakwise) even when the weather is warm, since to be without one would be accounted a sign of poverty. The black felt hat is decorated with cowrie or mussel shells or even pieces of bone; it is bound with red or mauve and invariably has an eagle's feather or two stuck in the band.

The women wear flowered patterns, kerchiefs and bright necklaces. They have no stockings but wrap linen round their feet under the tied-on leather shoes, or go barefoot.

A typical costume suitable for *Oberek*—which originally was from the province of Mazovia (Mazowsze)—is a sleeveless coloured jacket, red, yellow and blue striped trousers tucked into riding boots. In Plate 2 the man has discarded his top coat and hat, which would be black with a touch of colour in the band. Farther south a small, squarish hat without a brim is worn, white, yellow or decorated with simple patterns. The woman's costume consists of a full striped skirt and apron and a close-fitting sleeveless bodice of bright hue over a fine white linen blouse. Coral necklaces are popular, and girls wear a coloured head-band or scarf, or an embroidered cap decorated with gay ribbons hanging down behind.

The *Mazur* also originates in Mazovia. A typical costume is a military jacket of bright blue and loose red trousers. The long coat is belted, the hat is square-crowned, the band of dyed sheepskin possibly decorated with a rosette of flowers and ribbons. Westwards in Poznań the man's attire is less brilliant and a black stovepipe hat is worn. The girls' head-dress in Mazovia is remarkable. They vie with one another in producing elaborations of ribbons and flowers, the success of this traditional fancy depending on the initiative of the wearer. High boots, necklace and ornamented apron add to the gaiety of the womenfolk. In Poznań head-dresses are less elaborate; a white linen coif, reminiscent of the Middle Ages, is incongruously decorated with flowers and ribbons. This coif was perhaps introduced amongst other things to Polish Hanseatic towns from far-away sister towns of the Hanseatic League in Holland during the fourteenth century, the gay decorations added by Polish taste.

The famous *Krakowiak* comes from the peasants of the region round Kraków. The man's dress is extremely showy, consisting of a long dark coat ornamented with red tassels, a wide belt from which swing a quantity of metal discs to clash and jingle, wide striped trousers tucked into top boots, and on his head a scarlet cap—somewhat like a Scottish Balmoral—with flying ribbons and soaring peacock's feathers. The woman wears her high laced boots, a yellow sleeveless coat over a white linen blouse, a flowered skirt and an entrancing head-dress thickly decorated with cut-out flowers and leaves, long floating ribbons swinging at the back. Her necklace is a valuable adornment.

OCCASIONS WHEN DANCING MAY BE SEEN

Between Christmas and Easter	Anywhere in the countryside when field work is slack.
Carnival, Zapusty	The chief day is the Thursday before Ash Wednesday.
Easter Monday	Practically everywhere. In towns passers-by squirt scent on the girls, in the country buckets of water are poured over them.
Whitsuntide	The 'Green Feast', when houses are decorated with green leaves and dancing takes place.
Corpus Christi	Religious processions with festivities afterwards.
St. John's Eve (June 23rd), Kupala	Midsummer fires on the hills, with jumping over them and dancing round them. Girls push floating garlands with lights on them into the river; men swim after them, to keep company with the girl.
Harvest Home, Dożynki	A great festival with dancing and music. On the last day of harvest a girl with a huge corn wreath on her shoulders and a crown on her head goes to the estate-owner, singing. He dances the first dance with her.

There are also home festivals, such as weddings and baptisms, which are never without dancing.

THE DANCES

TECHNICAL EDITORS
MURIEL WEBSTER AND KATHLEEN P. TUCK

*ABBREVIATIONS
USED IN DESCRIPTION OF STEPS AND DANCES*

r—right ⎫ referring to R—right ⎫ describing turns or
l—left ⎭ hand, foot, etc. L—left ⎭ ground pattern
C—clockwise C-C—counter-clockwise

For descriptions of foot positions and explanations of any ballet terms the following books are suggested for reference:

A Primer of Classical Ballet (Cecchetti method). Cyril Beaumont.

First Steps (R.A.D.). Ruth French and Felix Demery.

The Ballet Lover's Pocket Book. Kay Ambrose.

Reference books for description of figures:

The Scottish Country Dance Society's Publications. Many volumes, from Thornhill, Cairnmuir Road, Edinburgh 12.

The English Folk Dance and Song Society's Publications. Cecil Sharp House, 2 Regent's Park Road, London N.W.1.

The Country Dance Book I-VI. Cecil J. Sharp. Novello & Co., London.

POISE OF BODY

The head is held proudly, the body erect except in steps which demand a definite forward and backward movement of the body, as in Oberek. In the Mazur, the man leans forward when dancing Pas de Mazur but retains great strength of back and leg.

The characteristic feature of the men's dancing is the vigour of movement which gives a dynamic quality that cannot be notated. Their movements contrast with the more flowing ones of the women although they too, led by the men, can work up to a spirited form of dance. The steps as danced by the men are not only more vigorous than those of the women, they are also deeper and more earthbound, particularly in Holupiec and Pas de Mazur.

ARM GESTURES AND HOLDS

The holds are described in each dance separately. They vary according to the step, as shown in the Mazur, where alternative steps are given with their different holds.

The free arm may be held on the hip; the women sometimes hold their skirts. More usually the free arm of both dancers is held obliquely outward from the shoulder, arm straight (see sketch opposite). The term used in the dance notations to describe this position is 'arm raised'.

BASIC STEPS

Polonez (Polonaise)
　A stately walk, bending the supporting leg on every 3rd beat, at the same time sliding the other foot forward and raising it slightly off the ground.

Holupiec (Coup de Talon)
　Raise foot slightly in air to side, small-spring clipping heels together in air, to land on the same supporting foot, leaving the free leg still slightly raised sideways.

Cwal (Chassé Coupé)
　A gallop step forward, keeping the same foot in front or sideways.

Pas de Valse	*Beats*
Step slightly sideways on r foot.	1
Close l foot, on ball of foot, behind r foot.	2
Change weight on to r foot.	3
Repeat, beginning on l foot.	

Pas de Basque	
Spring to side on r foot.	1
Transfer weight on to l foot on ball in front of r foot.	2
Small stamp on r foot behind, changing weight.	3
Repeat, beginning on l foot.	

Pas Marché
>Like Pas de Valse with a small spring, travelling forward rather than sideways and forward.

Pas d'Oberek
>Like Pas Marché only much more vigorous, with a strong accent on the 1st beat. It is often accompanied by a strong forward and backward movement of body and arms.

Pas de Mazur

	Beats
Chassé forward on l foot with r leg extended.	1
Hold this position.	2
Hop on l foot with slight heel-beat, still holding r leg extended.	3
Slight hop off l foot, to repeat the step with a chassé forward on r foot.	and
	1
Continue as above. The woman's step is more flowing than that of the man, who accents the 1st and 3rd beats and takes a deeper chassé.	

Révérence
>Woman makes a court curtsey. Man steps back, relaxing back knee, inclining the body forward and sweeping the same arm as front foot across body.

KRAKOWIAK

Region Southern, originally region round Kraków. Plate 4.

Character Lively.

Formation Couple dance. One large or several small circles with an even number of couples in each. Man is on L of woman. Arms linked.

Dance	MUSIC Bars
STEP I: CIRCLE	A
a With slight spring open feet to side, toes and knees slightly turned in, knees relaxed [the '*and*' beat before Bar 1].	
Slight spring back to starting position, closing heels together [*beat 1*].	1–8
Repeat above, to dance it 8 times in all.	
All dance Cwał (gallop) steps to R in circle.	9–16
	B
b Repeat I*a*, dancing Cwał to L.	17–32
STEP II: BREAK CIRCLES	A
Man's r arm round back of partner's waist, her l hand on his r shoulder; outside arms raised. Couples dance Cwał steps forward, outside feet leading, moving into two large circles and on the last 2 bars dividing to make lines of four behind one another, dancers holding hands behind backs.	1–16

KRAKOWIAK

Arranged by Arnold Foster

Play 4 times

STEP III: LINES

a 6 Cwał steps to side, followed by 3 stamps; alternate lines to R, others to L.
Repeat back to places.
Repeat in opposite direction and back to places.

b Repeat IIIa.

STEP IV: FORM CIRCLES
Repeat Step II, dancing in one circle or several small circles, arms linked.

STEP V
Repeat Step I.

B
17–32

A
1–16

B
17–32

A–B
1–32

MAZUR

Region   Mazovia. Plate 1.

Character   Stately.

Formation   Couple dance, man on L of woman.

Dance

STEP I

Two steps may be used, either A (simple) or B (advanced).

A. 16 Pas marchés, travelling C in circle. The man holds the woman's l hand in his r hand, arms forward below shoulder line, his l hand on hip and her r hand holding skirt.

B. 1 Pas de Mazur on l foot, followed by 1 Pas marché on r foot. Repeat 7 times, travelling C in circle. The man has his r arm round woman's waist, her l hand in his l hand. He leans slightly forward ahead of his partner, looking at her all the time. The man's step is deeper and more strongly accented than that of the woman, which is more flowing.

Finish in line formation, three or four couples in each line, partners side by side and facing forward.

STEP II

4 Pas marchés on the spot, holding inside hands.

MUSIC
Bars
A
1–8
repeated

B
9–12

MAZUR

Arranged by Arnold Foster

Play twice through with repeats

The man leaps into the air and drops to a kneeling position on l knee, facing to R. He holds the woman's l hand in his r hand while she dances 4 Pas de Mazur C-C round him. He allows his r hand to pass overhead as he watches her dance. He stands up on the last beat.	13–16
Repeat; finish with partners facing one another, having let go hands.	9–16

STEP III   A

Both travel to L, r arm raised.

1 Holupiec (coup de talon) with l foot raised [*beat 1*].   1
Stamp on l foot [*beat 2*].
Hold position [*beat 3*].

Beat r foot without changing weight [*beat 1*].   2
Hold this position [*beats 2 and 3*].

Repeat to R, with l arms raised, finishing with weight on l foot. Partners place l arms round waists, l shoulders almost touching and r arms raised.   3–4

1 Holupiec with r foot raised sideways, followed by 2 stamps on r and l feet.   5

Repeat this sequence 3 times, turning C-C.   6–8

Repeat.   1–8

STEP IV   B

Repeat Step II. Just before the last beat partners clap own hands and spring into 4th position facing each other, the man holding the woman's l hand in his r hand, free arms raised.   9–16 repeated

Plate 3   Góralski

GÓRALSKI

(*Brigand dance from the mountains*)

Region	Podhale (Zakopane). Plate 3.
Character	Strong and lively.
Formation	Solo or group dance for men, who hold the *toporek* or small axe in their hands. The women may dance Step III, remaining in a group in the background watching Steps I and II. If danced by men only, Steps III and IV would be omitted—half the group of men dancing Steps I and II, followed by the other half. These two steps would be repeated.

Dance

	MUSIC Bars
STEP I The men skip C-C to form a circle, holding *toporki* above heads. They continue to skip when the circle is formed, turning body slightly to centre of circle and making cutting movement with *toporek*. The cutting movement traces a figure of 8. During the last 2 bars skip to face forward if a solo; into lines to face each other, if a group dance.	A 1–8 B 9–16
STEP II With slight spring bend both knees, kicking heels in air [*beat* 1].	A 1

GÓRALSKI

Play 4 times

Small jump on l foot, lifting r foot up behind, slapping r foot with l hand [*beat* 2].

Repeat on alternate feet, changing *toporek* into the other hand with a small throw on each knee-bend. | 2–8

STEP III | B
Men saunter or Cwał (gallop) in a semicircle and watch women, who dance 8 Pas de Basque into the centre of the semicircle, free hands on hip. | 9–16

The women then dance 2 Pas de Basque on the spot, 2 turning R about. Repeat. | A 1–8

The women dance 8 Pas de Basque, moving back into semicircle. | B 9–16

STEP IV | A
Men dance forward into lines with 8 Pas de Basque. | 1–8

STEP V | B
Repeat Step II. | 9–16

Repeat the whole dance if desired.

OBEREK

Region	Mazovia. Plate 2.	
Character	Gay and vigorous.	
Formation	Couple dance.	

Dance	MUSIC *Bars*
STEP 1	
In twos, facing forward; the man's r hand round the back of his partner's waist, her l arm resting lightly on his shoulders and the free arm raised. Start with outside foot.	
a 1 Pas d'Oberek forward with vigorous arm and body movement forward and downward.	1
1 Pas d'Oberek backward, with arm and body movement upward and backward.	2
Repeat this forward and backward movement four and a half times (11 Pas d'Oberek in all), with a springy movement on the 1st beat.	3–11
Instead of the final movement all stamp on inside foot [*beat 1*]. Hold position [*beat 2*].	12
1 Holupiec [*beat 3*] raising outside leg, followed by 2 stamps [*beats 1 and 2*].	12–13
Repeat Holupiec and 2 stamps three times, turning to L throughout. Free arms are raised.	13–16
N.B.—The Holupiec always comes on the 3rd beat of a bar.	
b Repeat all.	17–32

OBEREK

Arranged by Arnold Foster

Play 3 times

STEP II
Partners release hold and face forward.

a Step towards one another on nearest foot, the man pushing the woman's l shoulder forward with his r shoulder, both raising outside feet.	1
Partners step on outside foot moving away from, but looking towards, one another and raising inside foot just off ground.	2
Repeat this swaying movement.	3–4
12 Pas marchés round in circle, casting away from partner.	5–16
b Repeat all.	17–32

STEP III
Repeat Step I*a*.   1–16

STEP IV

Man's r arm round partner's waist, her l arm through his r arm to give support (see Plate 2).

Man's Step.—1 Pas d'Oberek, starting with r foot and moving forward. | 17

Spring on l foot, turning half to R, hitting ground with l hand [*beat 1*] (see sketch), r leg extended backward, l toe touching ground, and knee well bent [*beat 2*]. | 18

Spring feet together with half-turn to R, landing with knees bent (demi plié), facing forward [*beat 3*].

Repeat the Pas d'Oberek and the turning step 6 times. | 19–30

Woman's Step.—14 Pas d'Oberek, starting r foot and turning with the man, leaning well away but assisting him on the spring with feet together. | (17–30)

Both dance 1 Pas d'Oberek, facing forward and bending forward. | 31

1 strong stamp, to finish with outside arms raised, man's r arm round woman's waist, her l hand on his shoulder. | 32

PRONUNCIATION

Every word has the stress on the penultimate syllable.

A is pronounced as in 'f*a*ther'; E as in 'm*e*n'; I as in 'pol*i*ce'; o as in 'm*o*re'.

ó and U are both as the English U in 'r*u*le'.

Y is as in 'p*i*ty', but pronounced with the lips rounded.

Ą as in French 'b*on*'; Ę as in French 'b*ien*'.

C is like the TS in 'bi*ts*'. It is never pronounced K.

Ć as in 'be*t y*ou', or in the old-fashioned pronunciation of 'na*t*ure' (*nay-tyoor*, not *nay-tcher*). CI before a vowel expresses the same sound, the I being there only to indicate the softening (palatalisation).

CZ is the English CH in '*ch*at'.

CH as in Scottish 'lo*ch*'.

G is always hard as in '*g*et'.

J is the English Y as in '*y*et'.

L as in '*l*eft'. There is also a 'hard l', spelt Ł, pronounced as in 'sha*ll*' but formed even farther back in the mouth; it can sound almost like the English w.

Ń as in 'mi*ni*on', or more exactly as in French 'mi*gn*on'.

S is always unvoiced as in '*s*it'.

Ś is palatalised, as in the old-fashioned pronunciation of 'fi*ss*ure' (*fiss-yoor*, not *fisher*). SI before a vowel is pronounced the same.

SZ is pronounced as the English SH.

W as English V; at the end of a word, as F.

Ź is palatalised, as in 'a*s y*ou were'. ZI before vowel is the same.

Ż and RZ have the sound of the s in 'plea*s*ure'.

37

BIBLIOGRAPHY

BAERLEIN, HENRY.—*No Longer Poles Apart.* London, 1936.
FIRSOFF, V. A.—*The Tatra Mountains.* London, 1942.
KURYLO, EDWARD DE.—'All about the Mazur.' *The Dancing Times,* Dec. 1938, Jan. and Feb. 1939.
LEWITT, J., and G. HIM.—*Polish Panorama.* London, 1941. (Contains photographs of instruments and costume.)
LOBACZEWSKA, STÉPHANIE.—'Les Danses polonaises.' *Archives Internationales de la Danse,* Paris, II, no. 1, 1934. (Illustrated.)
MANN, KATHLEEN.—*Peasant Costume in Europe.* Revised ed. London: A. & C. Black, 1950. (Coloured plates.)
MIERZEJEWSKA, JADWIGA.—*Teatr z Pieśni.* Warsaw, 1933. (Dances, diagrams, dance-songs.)
MIKULA, MARJAN.—*Dożynki.* Kraków, 1934. (Dances, diagrams, dance-songs, illustrations.)
—— *Sobotka.* Kraków, 1934. (Dances, diagrams, dance-songs.)
SUPER, PAUL.—*The Polish Tradition.* London, 1939.
TILKE, MAX.—*The Costumes of Eastern Europe.* London, 1926. (Illustrated.)
TYSZKIEWICZ, A., et al.—*Polish Folk Dances and Dance-Songs.* London: Polish Army Education Bureau, [c. 1940].

Plate 4 *Krakowiak*

www.ingramcontent.com/pod-product-compliance
Lightning Source LLC
Chambersburg PA
CBHW061744290426
43661CB00127B/974